THE MIDDLE SCHOOL SURVIVAL
HANDBOOK™

NAVIGATING
A NEW SCHOOL

TERRY TEAGUE MEYER

rosen publishing's
**rosen
central®**

NEW YORK

To Carolyn and Susan

Published in 2013 by The Rosen Publishing Group, Inc.
29 East 21st Street, New York, NY 10010

Library of Congress Cataloging-in-Publication Data

Meyer, Terry Teague.
Navigating a new school/Terry Teague Meyer.—1st ed.
    p. cm.—(The middle school survival handbook)
Includes bibliographical references and index.
ISBN 978-1-4488-8312-7 (library binding)—
ISBN 978-1-4488-8319-6 (paperback)—
ISBN 978-1-4488-8320-2 (6-pack)
1. Middle school students—United States—Juvenile literature.
2. Middle schools—United States—Juvenile literature.
3. Articulation (Education)—United States—Juvenile literature.
4. First day of school—United States—Juvenile literature. I. Title.
LB1623.5.M497 2013
373.236--dc23

2012018548

Manufactured in the United States of America

CPSIA Compliance Information: Batch #W13YA: For further information, contact Rosen Publishing, New York, New York, at 1-800-237-9932.

CONTENTS

INTRODUCTION

Moving up from elementary school to a larger middle school is cause for excitement. Middle school offers more freedom and choices. Students get to walk down the hall and talk to friends on the way to class. Middle school probably means a schedule of different teachers and classmates and a wide array of school activities.

But the transition to middle school also brings new challenges and responsibilities. Having different teachers means needing to keep track of added routines and demands. The freedom to get to class at your own pace means having to figure out how to get there on time, with the right book and notebook. Students must now navigate unfamiliar hallways and staircases in a much bigger school.

The other students will be bigger, too. Many incoming middle school students wonder if they will be safe in their new school. They worry about bullies. Just fitting in is another concern. Those who have moved from a different area, town, or state may feel completely lost, far away from old friends and familiar

Moving up to middle school is an exciting time, full of nervousness and uncertainty but also anticipation and discovery.

surroundings. Those who have moved a long way or just made the next step up to middle school want to look and feel comfortable in the new school, not wander around looking bewildered and scared.

Confidence comes from knowing what lies ahead. Students about to enter middle school for the first time and those moving to a new school should be prepared. They should know what to expect before they begin middle school, on the first day of classes, and then daily routines, including getting to and from school and after-school activities. Any questions about navigating middle school and dealing with problems that often come up during this time of change and transition should be answered. How do you get to class on time with everything you need? Will old friends from elementary school still be there? How can someone new to the area make new friends? How do you organize and juggle different classes and find time for extracurricular activities?

We'll focus on avoiding problems in daily situations like getting to and from school, navigating the school and its hallways, and organizing books, homework, lockers, and time. We'll cover social issues like the awkwardness of gym locker rooms, finding someone to sit with at lunch, and widening your circle of friends. Readers will get pointers on dealing with academic and social pressure and where to get good information and help when it's needed. Knowing the importance of planning ahead is an excellent beginning. So let's get started with some strategies to make your transition to a new middle school as smooth as possible.

CHAPTER ONE

GETTING READY FOR THE FIRST DAY OF SCHOOL

What will your middle school look like? Those moving to a new school from far away will want to know first what grades are included in the school. This and more information is available directly from the school or school district. Often it can be found online.

The terms "middle school" and "intermediate school" describe schools that, like young people, come in all shapes and sizes. Junior high school typically includes grades seven through nine, including the freshman year of high school. Middle schools that feed into four-year high schools often cover grades six through eight. Some students end up attending two different middle schools—one for fifth and sixth grades and another for seventh and eighth. This can be both good and bad news. Students have to learn their way around an additional building, but they get to be top dogs (and underdogs!) twice. Of course,

Middle schools come in all shapes and sizes. Touring your school in advance, as these students are doing, will help you find your way around the first day.

those who live in a very small town or attend a private school may not actually move to a new campus. For some, the transition to middle school may simply involve a move upstairs or to an adjacent building.

Because school principals and teachers want incoming students to succeed, most schools offer some form of orientation program. The word "orientation" is related to finding a sense of direction. When you orient yourself, you're making sure that you are headed in the right direction in a new situation. Orientation may take many forms. Principals or counselors and even current middle school students may visit your elementary school to talk about what to expect. At some point, transitioning students will likely visit the new school. There may be several opportunities to visit.

The Middle School Guidance Counselor

Chances are, the first part of your orientation to the new school will be in the form of a visit from guidance counselors who will explain curriculum requirements (what you must study) and elective choices. School guidance counselors—people who guide and give counsel (advice)—are actively involved in students' lives in middle school. Since students are taking a mixture of required

School guidance counselors help students map out their academic futures. They can also assist with personal and social issues.

and elective courses, guidance counselors must make up a personal schedule for each student. Parents are usually involved in this process. Often counselors will have meetings with individual students and parents to develop an overall plan of study throughout middle school in preparation for high school.

Schools match up counselors and students in a variety of ways. Some counselors divide up the students alphabetically. Someone with the last name Adams, for example, will work with the counselor who has the A through E students throughout his or her years at the school. In this system, families with several children will become familiar with that one guidance counselor over time. Other schools assign counselors by grade level, so that the sixth-grade counselor is a real expert in the problems and needs of sixth graders (which differ from those of eighth graders). Whatever system the school uses, the counselor is important to every middle school student. Guidance counselors are experts in understanding young people and are there to help students succeed.

Orientation

After a visit from the administrators (principal and assistant principals) and guidance counselors, incoming students will likely visit their new school either in the spring or summer before classes begin. Ideally, there will be more than one visit. A tour of the school will give an idea of distances from the cafeteria to the classroom and gym. The guide will likely discuss important information about getting around—for example, if certain staircases are used for traffic in only one direction. The more time students have to get familiar with the new school, the more at home they will feel on the first day. Some schools are open for a few hours before the school year begins so entering students (including those new to the area) can walk around with their schedules in hand and figure out how to get from one place to another. Be sure to take advantage of this if you can because the halls will be crowded and it will be harder to find your way around on the first day of school. Some summer orientation sessions will include things like the opportunity to get a school-issued lock or gym clothes and to find out about clubs and school activities.

What if you are moving from another school district or city and miss out on the orientation sessions that took place before you

Students and parents tour the local middle school during orientation. This is an excellent opportunity to get answers to questions about rules, policies, class locations, building layout, daily schedules, clubs, sports, extracurriculars, and many other topics of interest.

arrived? When your parents enroll you in the school, have them ask about getting a tour. The counselor or registrar (the person who keeps records of students and their grades) probably has an information packet prepared just for new students. Schools want new students to feel at home, so they often provide "student ambassadors" (students familiar with the school) to serve as guides and mentors to new students. Schools and school districts also publish newsletters and orientation information to be mailed out. Students moving to a new school or district can call and request this information. Look for other community resources online or have your parents ask their realtor or rental agent to obtain desired information. Organizations such as Boy Scouts and Girl Scouts, Rotary, and religious groups offer opportunities outside the school to welcome you to a new community.

Don't overlook the Internet as a resource. Long before you move to a new school, information is available online. Schools and individual teachers often have Web sites and Web pages, which can tell a lot about a new school. Pictures of the building and school year and school day calendars are posted online. The school Web site may even include a map of the building. If you are having a hard time deciding on an elective, you can likely find information about available choices, including music groups and team sports.

At orientation, or on the first day of school, students may receive an agenda (school planner)—a special notebook with the school calendar and other important information, followed by pages for daily entries of homework assignments for each class throughout the year. If the school does not provide such a planner, you should buy one along with other school supplies. Organization is essential in making a smooth transition to middle school.

ELECTIVES

Middle school students get to choose some of what they study. Of course everyone will have to take the basics: language arts, math, science, and social studies. But there will likely be choices, too. Some middle schools offer a rotating schedule of electives (classes you "elect" or choose), and students try out each one for a few weeks. Music, art, life skills, metal and wood shop (or "industrial arts"), and foreign languages are typical offerings.

This kind of arrangement is like going to a cafeteria to sample several new dishes and decide what you like. In some cases, the chosen elective will be taken for a semester (half a year) or even for the whole year. Such scheduling is great for those who already know they would like to study art, learn a musical instrument, or take up acting. You may be able to sample a series of foreign languages or begin studying just one in depth. Beginning to learn a foreign language in middle school means that you'll be able to continue in high school and really learn to read, write, and speak it fluently by the time you graduate.

Much like a team sport, an elective that involves performing (band, orchestra, chorus, or theater arts) brings together students who share an interest in the same activity and rehearse as a group. That's kind of like having an instant group of new friends. Choosing electives can definitely have an important impact on that first year in middle school.

The First Day of School

The first day of school is always full of excitement and some confusion. Bus schedules may still be a mystery to everyone, so it's a good idea to arrive at the stop early. Many parents bring their students to school the first day, even if they plan to use a school bus or public transportation later.

Many students wear new clothes or a favorite outfit on the first day of school. They want to feel confident and make a good impression. It's a good idea to check the school dress code to be sure of what is acceptable. Orientation information or the school district Web site will include a list of what not to wear.

Preparing for the first day of school is especially exciting when you are moving to a new school or campus. Many students feel more confident if they take the time to look their best.

Once at school, you'll find administrators and teachers prepared to prevent confusion by stationing lots of people at entrances and hallways to monitor activity and answer questions. Although many students already have class schedules, everyone will likely get a final updated schedule on the first day. There will be signs directing where to go and maps to help. Students will be directed to pick up schedules by grade or alphabetic order.

If your middle school includes only fifth and sixth grades, you likely do not have a different teacher for every class, although you'll probably have more than one. Chances are, your schedule will not seem very different from elementary school. The first day of school means going to your classroom, where you will receive most of the information you need.

Many students buy school supplies before school starts. Some schools put together packets of supplies and sell them to raise funds for the school. It is best not to bring supplies the first day, other than something to write on and write with. Bring some kind of folder as well, as you'll undoubtedly get lots of papers to take home, many of which must be signed by a parent or guardian and returned to school. Whether or not you bring a backpack or book bag the first day will depend on when lockers are assigned and when books will be issued.

Even students who have walked the halls before may find it confusing to move from class to class, so don't be afraid to ask someone for help. Most buildings are arranged by subjects, with specific areas of the school devoted to science, math, social studies, language arts, etc. This is convenient, but it also means that upon leaving math class, the student will probably have to walk a good distance to get to the band

Don't buy school supplies until you are sure what you will need. Many teachers have very detailed requirements.

hall. A room marked "T" or "annex" is probably located in a "temporary" building outside the main one. If you have had a chance to explore the building or study a map beforehand, you may already know your way around. If not, don't hesitate to ask the teachers, principals, and volunteers in the hall. It's good to know that most schools don't count a student tardy during the first week of school.

The first day of school most teachers will talk a great deal about their expectations for study habits and behavior in class. They will likely hand out written information for your parents to sign. This is the time to get out the planner and start writing down dates when signed papers and supplies are due. It might seem hard to absorb all the different information throughout the day, so it's a good idea to reread your notes and handouts at home. Unless the school has provided a specific list of school supplies, you may discover the first day why it's best to wait to buy them. Many teachers (who need to be super organized to keep track of all their students) are very picky about what type or color of folders and notebooks they require.

Lunchtime goes by very fast on the first day of school. Bringing a lunch on the first day (or the entire first week) will leave time to scout out food choices, look for old friends (to share new experiences with), and eat without feeling too rushed. Remember to look around the cafeteria for information about bus schedules and extracurricular activities, which may be posted during lunch.

At the end of the first day, whether it was super or scary, you can congratulate yourself on being an official middle school student.

CHAPTER TWO

GETTING TO AND FROM SCHOOL

How you get to school—school bus, car, or public transportation—may change as you move to a middle school that is larger and farther away than before. The mode of transportation will depend on your distance from school and your surroundings (city, suburbs, or small town). But any means of getting to school raises safety and social issues. And certain safety precautions apply to students of all ages, who should always be aware of their surroundings, stay in groups, avoid strangers, and stay on the most direct, familiar route to school or the bus stop.

Public Transportation

Students who live in densely populated cities will likely use the subway or city buses to get to and from school. In some instances, students may have chosen to attend a school far from home because they want to take advantage of special programs or simply a better school. Urban students already know how to use public transportation and are familiar with basic safety guidelines (travel with a buddy, don't talk to strangers, and be

Students using public transportation to get to school should plan out the route and take a few test runs before the first day.

aware of when it's your stop). To gain confidence and learn how much time your daily trip will take, make several trial runs getting to and from school before the school year starts. A parent, sibling, or older friend could go along the first time. Have someone time your first solo trip.

The School Bus

Many parents take their kids to school the first day because of uncertainty about bus routes. Your orientation materials may include bus route information. If not, this will be available the first day of school. Look for bus routes posted in the cafeteria or in your information packet. During the first week of school, bus

Get to know the people at your bus stop. You will spend a lot of time with them and may make some strong, lasting, and valuable friendships.

schedules may be hard to figure out, partly because the school may be adjusting routes as they discover how many students in a given neighborhood actually ride.

Missing the school bus can be a big hassle, so plan to arrive at your stop early. This may mean a long wait early in the school year, but it will likely shorten as drivers become more familiar with their routes. Before you even take the bus, prepare a plan in case you miss it. If you have a cell phone, know whom to call (you don't want to call the parent who is already on the way to work). This could be a parent who works from home, a neighbor, or a friend's parent. If you don't have a cell phone, make arrangements in advance with a neighbor who will be home in case you need to call the school or your parents.

Bus Stop Etiquette

The school day really starts at the bus stop, where you'll likely be joined by neighbor kids. If you are new to the area or don't know them, introduce yourself, as you may be spending a fair amount of time together. Consider this time an opportunity to make friends and relax before school. However, if you are harassed or bullied by anyone at the bus stop or while riding, report it to a teacher or administrator once you get to school. Younger students who feel intimidated riding with older kids may want to sit up front, closer to the driver, if seats are available. Once on the bus, visit with your friends, but try to keep

The ride to and from school is a good time to visit and catch up with friends. Have fun, but observe the rules and keep the noise down in order not to distract your bus driver.

the noise level down. The driver will appreciate it. Don't linger around the bus stop after being dropped off in the afternoon. If your fellow bus riders have become friends, make plans to get together at someone's home.

Students involved in sports, clubs, or other activities that meet after school will need to make special arrangements to get home. Note meetings and practices in your daily planner so that alternative transportation can be arranged in advance. Imagine heading home on the bus only to remember there's a drama club meeting going on back at school. Carpooling from these activities will ease the burden on parents and provide the opportunity to get to know the other students. Early in the school year, look for students from your neighborhood or ask around. The coach or club sponsor may have information on where students live. Once carpool arrangements are set, remember the importance of getting to the ride as quickly as possible and not leaving everyone

DAILY CAR POOLS

For some students, carpooling makes sense as the best way to get to and from school. In the morning or after school, the most important rule for car pools is to be on time. This is true for drivers (your parent) as well as students. Be thoughtful of others and eat breakfast before getting into the car to avoid making a mess (or making others jealous!). A second rule is to inform the driver in advance if illness or an after-school activity prevents you from riding on a given day.

waiting for you. If you take public transportation, let your family know to expect you home later on certain days.

Walking or Biking to School

For students who walk or bike to school, safety is of primary importance. Bike riders should wear helmets at all times and use bike lanes wherever possible. Allow enough time to lock your bike in the appropriate location when you get to school. If you are an occasional bike rider, you might need to note in your planner which days are which. Sometimes students forget how

Biking to school can be fun and a great source of exercise. Just remember to observe all local safety codes and road rules.

they came to school and leave bikes in the bike rack overnight, exposing them to theft and bad weather.

Walkers and bike riders alike are safer in pairs or small groups. Your parents have undoubtedly talked to you about avoiding strangers. A group is less likely to be approached than a student walking alone. Also for safety reasons, avoid shortcuts through areas not visible from the street and stay on streets with plenty of people. Of course, walkers should stay on the sidewalks wherever possible and use the available guarded crossings. As with a car pool, it's important to meet your transportation group on time or let them know ahead of time if you can't join them.

CHAPTER THREE

LOCKER LOGISTICS

School policies on lockers and backpacks vary widely. Many schools do not allow students to carry backpacks throughout the day. Crowded hallways make it tough to move quickly, and no one wants to be accidentally body-slammed by someone else's backpack! Not to mention, books are heavy. Some schools require students to lock their belongings in a locker. The school may even issue locks and not allow students to bring their own. Other schools assign lockers but don't allow locks. Students in these schools obviously can't store valuables in their lockers.

Get Organized!

Organization is the key to locker logistics. First off, make sure your backpack will fit in the locker. At the end of the first day of classes, study your map of the school to see if you got from place to place the quickest and most direct way. Once books are issued, you'll know how much they weigh and when you'll need each one. With this information, you can plan how many times during the day you'll need to go to your locker

Keeping assignments and books organized will make it easier to adjust to having to shift among several different teachers and classrooms throughout the day.

to drop off and pick up books and notebooks. Try to factor in gym clothes and bathroom breaks at the same time. After a week or so, look at your daily routine again and see if you can improve further on it.

Since there's not enough time between classes to search through a messy locker, keep it tidy. There are locker shelves available to prevent everything from ending up in a heap. Color coding can help organize materials for each class. Textbook covers (probably required by the school) can be personalized so that yours don't look like everyone else's. Cover each book in a distinctive way to easily tell them apart. Cover your math textbook to match the color of your math notebook and then simply reach for the red (or blue or pink) book and notebook. Also, it's easier to grab the books you need if you store them standing straight up and down in the locker (instead of lying flat on top of each other). Write your name and school year in all textbooks (if there's a place provided), and write down your textbook numbers at home, along with your locker combination. Doing this might save your parents money if someone decides to steal your book to replace one that was lost!

If your teacher didn't require you to have certain types of notebooks or folders, come up with your own system to keep track of your things. For example, you might have a green folder and/or notebook for science, blue ones for English, and so on. If there isn't time at the end of class to get everything in the right place, consider having an "everything folder" (of a different color or design) to sort through at the end of each day. The danger of this system is that the "everything folder" is actually the bottom of a locker or backpack and the papers never get filed in their proper places. Middle school teachers can't keep handing

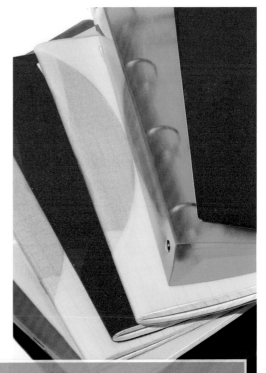

Color coding books and notebooks will help you keep track of what needs to be brought to each class and where assignments and homework for each class can be found.

out the same project information again and again, so they may not offer duplicates of assignment sheets and calendars.

If you do use an "everything folder," sort through it every day, write down long-range assignments and projects in your planner, and bring home papers to be signed by your parents. To avoid still more folders, consider putting incoming (from school)

LOCKER DOS AND DON'TS

Don't bring anything valuable to school. Lockers are not completely safe even when locked. But if your school allows or requires locks, use them. In order not to lose time struggling with a lock between classes, you need to make dialing the combination feel like second nature. Write down the combination as soon as you get it and store the information in several different places, including somewhere at home. Give your parents a copy, along with your list of book numbers. Practice opening the lock until it becomes so easy you can do it without thinking.

Never share your locker combination with another student. Locks and lockers are famous targets of practical jokes like switching locks (known in Texas as a "dragonfly") and turning locks over to make them very hard to open (called a "butterfly"). By not sharing the combination and not leaving the dial on any number of the combination, students can outsmart pranksters. If for whatever reason a lock can't be opened, seek help from a teacher or administrator (who is likely monitoring the halls). They know this can happen and have keys to unlock school-issued locks. Failing that, bolt cutters can cut them open.

information on the left side of each folder and outgoing (back to school) ones on the right side, and always keep the most recent handouts on top of older ones. It sounds like extra bother at first, but this will soon become a habit that will save time otherwise wasted looking for misplaced materials.

Staying on top of assignments and homework is just as important as keeping up with gym clothes, books, and notebooks. Many middle school teachers make a point of teaching organizational skills along with subject matter. Some give "planner quizzes," which you can ace just by having old assignments written down (something that you should do every day). Fortunately, teachers often provide backup by including homework assignments and project information on a school Web site. An additional backup would be a "homework buddy" to call in case you missed an assignment. Find someone in each class during the first week of school and exchange contact information. Having a homework buddy is also a way to make a new friend.

Life in the Locker Room

Middle school gym class will be more structured than in elementary school. For starters, students may have to wear special clothes either purchased by parents or issued by the school. It's the student's responsibility to make sure that the gym outfit comes home regularly for washing and goes back to school on Monday. To help remember this, just imagine having to wear sweaty clothes after they've been stewing in a locker over the weekend. If necessary, write down "laundry" along with other weekend homework assignments. Consider buying two gym uniforms so that one is always clean and ready to go.

Middle school gym class will likely require changing clothes in the locker room. This may feel awkward at first, but everyone else feels the same way and it will soon become routine.

For some students, changing for gym class is a little intimidating. If you are modest and nervous about changing clothes around your peers, you are probably not alone. The best plan is to concentrate on changing quickly (there isn't much time, anyway). Others are likely doing the same. You probably won't have to take a shower in middle school; many middle schools don't even have showers. However, it's a good idea to bring deodorant and use it after working out. Since there isn't much time to change, avoid earrings or necklaces that might catch on your clothes and slow you down or even damage a sweater. If gym lockers are provided, make sure belongings are securely locked.

Locker room mischief and bullying are common features in teen television shows and movies, but not so much in real life. There is little time for pranks, as gym teachers want to maximize your time playing or working out. However, students who see or personally suffer from bullying should report it to the gym teacher or an administrator as soon as possible. Teachers and staff have the authority and know-how to deal with it quickly and effectively.

MYTHS and Facts

MYTH Bullying is everywhere in middle school and teachers do nothing to stop it.

Fact While bullying is more common in middle school than in elementary school, teachers, administrators, and guidance counselors are all trained to spot it and deal with it effectively. Always seek out a responsible adult as soon as you experience or witness bullying. Don't try to deal with it by yourself. Teachers and school officials have the authority and know-how to deal with it quickly and effectively.

MYTH With so many different teachers assigning homework and giving tests, it will be impossible to keep up with the schoolwork.

Fact Middle school will definitely be more academically demanding than elementary school. However, teachers are aware that students new to middle school need time to adjust to a greater workload. They try to teach organizational skills along with their subject matter. In many schools, teachers work in teams to plan lessons and projects so that they don't confuse or overwhelm students. Schools often have a system for ensuring that students don't have too many tests on the same day (for example, science and English test on odd-numbered days, social studies and electives on even-numbered days).

MYTH Middle schools are so big and the schedules so complicated that it will be really hard to make contact with old friends and meet new people.

Fact After the first few days, when the school becomes more familiar, finding old friends won't seem so difficult. After the first day, you can compare schedules with your elementary school friends and figure out where your paths might cross. With so many students, there's a larger pool of possible new friends. Try reaching out to students in your classes early on.

CHAPTER FOUR

SURVIVING LUNCH

Middle school will likely provide more freedom and choices at lunchtime than elementary school. Orderly lines of students may be replaced by disorganized lines forming around several food stations and a multiplicity of food choices, but no extra time to deal with them. Experienced students agree it's best to take your lunch to school for the first week. This will give you time to familiarize yourself with menu choices, prices, and the length of the lines. You'll also have more time available each day to find old friends or new classmates to sit with.

Since there's no recess, lunchtime is the best opportunity to unwind and visit with others. Of course, actually eating is important, too, since the school day is only half over. In recent years, schools are helping students make better food choices by limiting the availability of junk food. It's important to make wise choices when buying lunch. Double french fries and a giant soft drink do not make a meal, and they won't give you the energy and brain power you need to excel in school. Those who choose

Eating a good lunch will help maintain your energy level and brain power throughout the day. Whether you buy your lunch or make it yourself at home, try to make healthy and nutritious choices.

to buy lunch can usually preview menu choices on the school Web site or posted in the cafeteria at the beginning of the week.

Cafeteria Etiquette

No one ever complained about having too much time for lunch. Everyone is in a hurry. Consequently, students should be prepared by deciding what they want before reaching the front of the line. It's also important to know the cost and have your money ready. In recent years, more schools are using prepaid accounts that require students to enter a PIN (personal identification number)

IS THIS SEAT TAKEN?

Finding a place to sit and people to sit with can be a problem, especially if you are new to the school. Those who have grown up in the area can look for people they recognize from elementary school (even if they didn't actually know them), but newcomers will have to be proactive. Look around for faces you recognize from your new classes or the school bus.

Don't hesitate to introduce yourself to classmates as someone new to the school or the area. When you are new to a situation, it seems as if everyone else is in familiar surroundings. By telling people you are new, you might find other recent arrivals who are also eager to make new friends.

Lunch is a great time to relax and socialize. After a few days or weeks, you will probably find a group of pals to regularly eat lunch with.

Rather than stand around waiting for an invitation to join a group, simply go to an empty space and ask if the spot is taken. If someone says that the seat is being saved, move on and don't take it personally. Probably, the seat really is being saved. Obviously, you can't do this more than once or twice or there'll be no time to eat. Rather than break into a group conversation, be on the lookout for students who aren't talking to others. They are probably hoping for lunch companions. Don't worry if you don't find a group you really like to sit with during the first week of school—the problem should resolve itself as you make new friends.

at checkout. This system solves the problem of having to carry money around school, but it also requires remembering the PIN and noticing when the account is almost empty. Cafeteria workers will usually alert you when money should be added to the

Many schools now have automated systems for purchasing lunch, eliminating the need to carry cash.

account. There may also be a short-term loan possible for those whose accounts run too low.

Don't be someone who cuts in line or allows others to cut. Helping a friend this way is sure to make enemies of everyone behind you. Those who bring lunch from home won't have to deal with lines, but they will have to plan to get their lunch to school and to the lunchroom. That's something else to factor in when planning trips to and from your locker. Just in case, keep a little money in your school account or have cash on hand so you won't have to beg or starve if your lunch doesn't make it to school.

Be sure to clean up your space at the table and throw away and recycle your lunch waste in the appropriate containers. Don't leave a mess for the cafeteria staff to clean up after you.

CHAPTER FIVE

YOUR SOCIAL LIFE

Everyone wants to make a good impression on teachers and other students on the first day of school. That first day, students will be looking for familiar faces from elementary school. Those new to the area should wear a smile and look for other friendly faces. Whether your homeroom is based on the alphabet or the fact that you are all taking Spanish, it's a source of potential friends.

Making Friends in Class

Homeroom and elective classes are probably the best places to meet new friends—homeroom because there's no pressure to do subject warm-up activities, and electives because they offer opportunities to get to know students who share your interests, often in a nonclassroom setting. Musical groups may travel to competitions and concerts; drama groups often work together after school to prepare skits and readings. Foreign language clubs meet to introduce you to the food and culture of the language being studied. In such cases, you can

After-school clubs bring together students who share common interests.

interact with others in a more relaxed setting than the regular classroom.

Academic subjects also offer opportunities to get to know fellow students. You might find your new best friend among teammates in gym class or as a lab partner in science. Teachers in every subject stress collaborative learning—working together in teams to compare ideas or complete projects. Teachers have many reasons for matching up students as they do. A team may be created by chance, or the teacher may match up students whose strengths and weaknesses complement each other. Teachers also change up groups just to give students the chance to know everyone in the class better. Cooperative learning is a great way to make new friends, so look at each group project as a new social adventure. Plus, if you try your best to cooperate with others in the group, your project will likely be successful.

Making Friends Outside of Class

Many middle schools offer clubs that bring together students with shared interests. Your new school may have a student newspaper, some form of student government, and clubs for people interested in things like chess, computers, and foreign cultures. In addition, many schools offer team sports that offer competition with other schools or with teams within the school. With such exciting new activities to explore, some students sign up for too many and then

Electives, team sports, and extracurriculars, like marching band, require your time and commitment, but they also offer opportunities to participate in competitions and special events away from school.

have to drop something in order to keep up with schoolwork. It's best to try out one or two new activities at first to be sure there's enough time for everything.

If you are new to the area, you can find new friends outside of school through national programs like Boy Scouts and Girls Scouts and through youth programs in churches, synagogues, and mosques.

When Older Friendships Begin to Change

We've talked a lot about making new friends, but what about existing friendships? Middle school is a time of growth and

Some friendships strengthen during middle school. Others fade as you grow and change. When friendships come to an end, it is very sad, but this is a normal part of growing up. Even when you begin to go your separate ways, honor your old friendships by continuing to treat each other with respect, compassion, and empathy.

change in mind and body. Longtime friends may drift apart as they grow and change at different rates and in different directions. Groups from elementary school will likely change or even break up altogether. In the same way, strong friendships formed in middle school may not last through high school. How does one manage the loss of a friend? Recognize first that no one has to be at fault. You may be growing apart simply because of differing interests and widening horizons. For example, someone who loved sports in elementary school may now consider the school orchestra a priority. That doesn't mean he or she no longer likes former teammates, just that there is less time for them.

SOCIAL NETWORKING

Social media is an increasingly popular way to communicate with others, but it's no substitute for face-to-face conversation. Online comments can lead to misunderstandings. At its worst, social media has been used to bully and harass students mercilessly. A good rule to follow is not to say anything online that you would not say in person. An even more important rule is the Golden Rule. Think about how you would feel if you received a message like the one you're writing before writing something to or about another person. Although schools have little or no control over their students' social media interactions, understand that online activity can have serious consequences at school and in your social life. Be aware that unkind or thoughtless remarks as well as revealing photos will almost certainly come back to haunt you.

It is best to be honest with friends about how you feel—whether you feel neglected or want to spend less time with people than you used to. But you can be honest without being unkind. Try to put yourself in the other person's position and think how you would feel before talking to someone. A parent, teacher, or counselor might help you sort out your feelings if you sense a friendship is ending or needs to end. Above all, try to deal with the situation personally. Social media is no place for breakups.

Under Pressure

Depending on the age at which you enter middle school, you may be thinking (a lot!) about the opposite sex. Or you may be experiencing romantic feelings for someone of your own

Some middle school students are interested in romance; others aren't ready yet. It's important to know that men and women can be friends without dating. Hanging out as a group of friends can provide some of the best times you'll have during your school years.

sex. In both cases, these new feelings are completely normal. Ballroom dancing classes and church or synagogue youth groups bring young people together and provide supervised situations for social interaction. Some students may start pairing up in "steady" relationships, but middle school is too early to get into a serious relationship. Most middle school students are just starting to feel romantic attraction for the first time. Some students may not be interested in that kind of social relationship yet. Every student wants friends, but many are not ready for boyfriends and girlfriends, and that's perfectly OK.

Peer pressure can be very strong in middle school. It's natural to want to fit in and feel accepted by classmates. However, it's best to hold on to what you feel is important. Middle school is a time to widen your horizons and experiment with new ideas and new friendships, but you don't have to become a new—or false—you in order to be like everyone else.

CHAPTER SIX

STAYING SAFE AND GETTING HELP

Incoming middle school students may worry about safety in an environment with greater freedom and the presence of some students who are much larger and more mature than others. Teachers and school administrators are also very aware of these differences and consequently make every effort to keep students safe on school property. In some areas, students may feel safer at school than in the wider neighborhood. We have already discussed common sense guidelines for getting to and from school safely—stay in groups, use bike lanes and designated crosswalks, and be aware of your surroundings.

Know the Policies and Rules

The school handbook contains information about measures in place to ensure school safety, as well as rules regarding student misbehavior and its consequences. Districts often adopt certain policies that apply to all schools in the district, from kindergarten through high school. Other policies apply only to certain schools. It is very important that parents and students be aware

Policies on cell phone use in schools—in and out of class—vary widely. It's important to be aware of and follow the rules at your school.

of these policies. Parents may be required to sign a statement saying they are familiar with school policies that they have read in a printed handbook or online. People moving from a different district should study these rules and policies carefully, as they may differ from those of the previous school district.

Not knowing the rules is no excuse when someone breaks one. National attention has focused on students who suffered serious consequences for what seem to be minor offenses. For example, in some cases, giving an aspirin to another student has been treated the same as handing out an illegal drug. Writing on school property with a permanent marker has been considered a

Metal detectors are in place in many schools to ensure student safety and to help guarantee that no weapons or other dangerous items enter the building.

serious offense akin to spray-painting graffiti on the school walls. A threat made "as a joke" can land a student in an alternative school. Such examples are the result of zero-tolerance policies in schools. No exceptions are granted for infractions of certain rules, no matter what the student's intent. Becoming familiar with policies on absences, tardiness, makeup exams, and cell-phone use can prevent both academic and discipline problems.

In recent years, there has been much concern over school safety. For this reason, visitors to the school probably need to sign in at the office, present an official form of identification, and wear name tags while in the school. Students are required to have regular fire drills. There may also be drills for natural disasters and lock-downs in case of emergency. These drills and procedures must be taken seriously.

Many middle schools use technology to help maintain safety. Cameras may monitor halls and gym locker rooms. Teachers will likely have an in-class phone or intercom so they can summon help quickly. Metal detectors are becoming more common in some areas. Some schools perform random locker searches with handheld metal detectors or drug-sniffing dogs. These measures are in place to ensure that students are protected both from intruders and other students.

Trust and Rely on Responsible Adults

Once in the school, you should rely on teachers and administrators if you find yourself in an unsafe situation. Students who are bullied—physically, verbally, or via the Internet—should speak up. Parents should be the first to know, along with counselors. They can contact school administrators. In recent years, antibullying has become a priority in schools. You should also report any student's threat to harm others or themselves; not doing so could have dire consequences.

School administrators are aware that gang activity can penetrate into middle schools. In an effort to counteract gang influence, schools may have antigang programs and adopt dress code rules that limit the ability of gangs to display their presence through clothing. Students who feel pressured to join a gang—or any group they might be compelled to join without complete freedom of choice—should immediately talk to a counselor.

OFF-CAMPUS TRIPS

Students participating in sports, musical groups, and academic competitions may have the opportunity to stay overnight at school or take an off-campus trip to compete or perform. These outings are a great way to get to know classmates and teammates away from the normal and sometimes restrictive routine of the school day. Of course, these outings will be chaperoned. Teachers, administrators, and parents will be there to make sure that everyone is safe and behaving properly. For students, these outings are fun and challenging. It's important for everyone to act with maturity. Student pranksters who cause trouble can be sent home. Even worse, they may cause trouble for their fellow students or the reputation of the school.

Where to Get Help

We have already discussed the importance of the school counselor in scheduling classes for each student. The school counselor is the person to turn to with almost any kind of problem, whether personal or school-related. The counselor is trained and experienced in dealing with the problems of young people. He or she may also be a gatekeeper for reaching out to others (tutors, social workers, special education resources) who can provide additional help. Often a student will feel more comfortable talking first to a trusted teacher, who can listen and refer him or her to an appropriate counselor if necessary.

Students should feel comfortable reaching out to teachers and counselors for help with academic or personal problems.

Students having trouble in a subject should definitely contact the teacher directly. With so many students, teachers can't know if or why a student is having difficulty without direct information. Students who failed to complete a project or do homework because they didn't understand the assignment or the ideas presented might appear to the teacher to be simply lazy, forgetful, or disorganized. Telling the teacher about the problem might lead to another way for him or her to explain the concept or offer a modified assignment or a chance for tutoring.

But what if the problem is the teacher? It's true—sometimes students and teachers simply don't get along. But complaining to friends and parents that someone just doesn't like you won't improve the situation. If you approach the teacher directly and ask how he or she thinks you can improve your performance or behavior, he or she will realize you care and will likely look at you in a more positive light. If the problem continues, you might then talk to your counselor and arrange a meeting with your teacher and a parent.

For academic problems, the counselor may also be able to provide useful tips on how to improve study habits and organizational skills to manage the larger middle school workload. A counselor may recommend testing for vision, hearing, or attention problems. For this, the counselor may refer the student to a diagnostician (an expert in determining the source of learning difficulties). The counselor might also refer someone to a social worker for help with problems associated with family relationships and economic difficulties. Help can also come from community resources like service clubs and religious organizations.

Don't hesitate to ask for extra help. A small amount of one-on-one time with a teacher can lead to learning breakthroughs and clear up any confusion that has been holding you back.

As in elementary school, the school nurse provides help when students become sick. They also deal with immunization records and medication for students who need it on a regular basis. Middle school infirmaries (the nurses' offices) sometimes provide more extensive services. Although nurses may not be able to provide over-the-counter drugs such as aspirin without parental permission, it's the best place to go for students who are feeling sick. Infirmaries also often provide emergency sanitary protection for girls having their periods and information about puberty.

10 GreAT QUESTiONS
TO ASK A TEACHER OR GUIDANCE COUNSELOR

1 How will I need to change my study habits so I can succeed in middle school?

2 How can I make new friends?

3 Where do I go for tutoring?

4 I love sports, but I'm not good enough to make the school team. Are there other athletic opportunities for people like me?

5 How can I deal with a teacher who seems not to like me?

6 How can I get to all my classes on time?

7 What should I do about bullies at the bus stop?

8 My books are too heavy to carry home at night. What can I do?

9 Can anyone at school help me with problems at home?

10 I'm uncomfortable about the way my body is changing. Who can I talk to at school?

academic Related to education or learning.

administrator The person responsible for running an organization or business. The principal and assistant principals are school administrators.

agenda A notebook for listing daily homework assignments and project due dates. Also called a planner or binder-reminder.

chaperone An adult who accompanies and monitors students on off-campus trips.

clique A small group of people who spend time together and exclude others from their group.

counselor A school adviser who guides students by offering advice about schedules, classes, and personal and academic problems.

curriculum What is studied at school. The term "core curriculum" refers to the basic and required courses in math, science, reading, writing, and social studies.

detention A form of punishment for tardiness or misbehavior. Students are required to spend time supervised before or after school or for an entire school day.

diagnostician A person who specializes in figuring out the cause of student learning and behavior problems. One diagnostician might work at several schools.

elective A class that a student freely chooses to take, rather than being required to take it.

extracurricular School-sponsored activities that occur outside the classroom, often after school. Sports and clubs would be examples of extracurricular activities.

infirmary The nurse's office at school. Also called a clinic. This is where students go who become sick at school. The school nurse may also test students' vision and hearing.

mentor A student or adult who provides advice and help to a student on a regular basis.

orientation A program of activities and information to help students become familiar with their new school before the beginning of the school year.

puberty The developmental period during which young people mature physically and become capable of reproduction.

registrar A school administrator who keeps records of grades and other student information. Students moving to a school will have to present records (transcripts) from their old school in order to register (enroll) at the new one. In smaller schools, the person who handles these tasks may also have others jobs, like handling attendance records.

service organizations Clubs outside the school, like Rotary International, that bring people together to carry out projects designed to help others within the community.

student government An organization in which elected students represent the interests and needs of the entire student body and help organize school projects and activities.

tutor A person who provides extra help to students having difficulty with school work. This may be a regular teacher who tutors outside of class, another student, or a paid or volunteer adult.

zero tolerance A policy that offers no allowances for breaking rules and involves punishment without exceptions for first offenses.

Association for Middle Level Education (AMLE)
4151 Executive Parkway, Suite 300
Westerville, OH 43081
(800) 528-6672
Web site: http://www.amle.org
This association provides support and resources to teachers
and others who work with middle school students. Its Web
site includes publications of interest to students and parents as well as teachers.

British Colombia Ministry of Education
P.O. Box 9045, Stn Prov Govt
Victoria, BC V8W 9E2
Canada
(888) 879-1166
Web site: http://www.gov.bc.ca/bced
Education in Canada is governed by a separate ministry of
education for each province. The British Colombia Ministry
of Education is typical. The ministry's Web site provides
information about the school system, curriculum, and current articles of interest.

Canadian Education Association (CEA)
119 Spadina Avenue, Suite 705
Toronto, ON M5V 2L1
Canada
(416) 591-6300
Web site: http://www.cea-ace.ca

The CEA is a cross-Canada network with a strong membership base of leaders in the education, research and policy, not-for-profit, and business sectors. It is committed to education that leads to greater student engagement; teaching that inspires students and teachers and that causes all students to learn; and schools that ensure both equity and excellence in pursuit of the optimal development of all students.

Great Schools, Inc.
160 Spear Street, Suite 1020
San Francisco, CA 94105
Web site: http://greatschools.org
This is a nonprofit organization whose mission is to inspire and guide parents to become effective champions of their children's education, both at home and in the community. The Web site provides articles and worksheets to help students academically and socially.

It's My Life
Corporation for Public Broadcasting Service (PBS)
401 Ninth Street NW
Washington, DC 2004-2129
(202) 849-9600
Web site: http://www.pbskids.org/itsmylife/school/middleschool
This Web site, funded by PBS, offers articles, videos, and games related to the social and academic concerns of middle school students.

StopBullying.gov
U.S. Department of Health & Human Services
200 Independence Avenue SW
Washington, DC 20201
Web site: http://stopbullyingnow.hrsa.gov
This Web site is managed by the Department of Health and
Human Services, along with the Departments of Education
and Justice. The site offers information in the form of arti-
cles, Webcasts, and links on how young people, adults, and
communities can deal with bullying and prevent it.

U.S. Department of Education
400 Maryland Avenue SW
Washington, DC 20202
(800) USA-LEARN (872-5327)
Web site: http://www.ed.gov
The U.S. Department of Education carries out a number of
functions. It is charged with collecting data on schools,
distributing federal financial aid, and ensuring equal access
to education. It offers subject-area publications to help
students succeed in school.

Web Sites

Due to the changing nature of Internet links, Rosen Publishing
has developed an online list of Web sites related to the subject
of this book. This site is updated regularly. Please use this link
to access the list:
http://www.rosenlinks.com/MSSH/Navi

Belfield, Annie, and Travis Clark. *A Guys' Guide to Stress/A Girls' Guide to Stress.* Berkeley Heights, NJ: Enslow Publishers, 2008.

Borgenicht, David, Robin Epstein, and Ben H. Winters. *Worse-Case Scenario Survival Handbook: Middle School* (Worse Case Scenario Junior Editions). San Francisco, CA: Chronicle Books, 2009.

Burns, Jan. *Friendship: A How-to Guide.* Berkeley Heights, NJ: Enslow Publishers, 2011.

Cook, Colleen Ryckert. *Frequently Asked Questions About Social Networking.* New York, NY: Rosen Publishing, 2011.

Fox, Annie. *Be Confident in Who You Are* (Middle School Confidential). Minneapolis, MN: Free Spirit Publishing, 2008.

Gephart, Donna. *How to Survive Middle School.* New York, NY: Delacourt, 2010.

Humphrey, Sandra McLeod. *Hot Issues, Cool Choices: Facing Bullies, Peer Pressure, Popularity, and Put-Downs.* Amherst, NY: Prometheus Books, 2007.

Jacobs, Thomas A. *Teen Cyberbullying Investigated: Where Do Your Rights End and Consequences Begin?* Minneapolis, MN: Free Spirit Publishing, 2010.

McPherson, Stephanie Sammartino. *Stressed Out in School? Learning to Deal with Academic Pressure.* Berkeley Heights, NJ: Enslow Publishers, 2010.

Mosatche, Harriet, and Karen Unger. *Too Old for This Too Young for That!: Your Survival Guide for the Middle School Years.* Minneapolis, MN: Free Spirit Publishing, 2010.

Moss, Haley. *Middle School—The Stuff Nobody Tells You About: A Teenage Girl with High-Functioning Autism Shares Her Experience.* Shawnee Mission, KS: Autism Asperger Publishing, 2010.

O'Connor, Frances. *Frequently Asked Questions About Academic Anxiety.* New York, NY: Rosen Publishing, 2007.

O'Dell, Kathleen. *Agnes Parker...Keeping Cool in Middle School.* New York, NY: Dial Books for Young Readers, 2007.

Tarshis, Thomas Paul. *Living with Peer Pressure and Bullying (Teen Guides).* New York, NY: Checkmark Books, 2010.

Akos, Patrick. "Extracurricular Participation and the Transition to Middle School." Association for Middle Level Education. Retrieved December 2011 (http://www.amle.org/portals/0/pdf/publications/RMLE/rmle_vol29_no9.pdf).

Allman, Toney. *Cliques.* Farmington Hills, MI: Lucent Books, 2011.

Almond, Lucinda, ed. *School Violence.* Farmington Hills, MI: Greenhaven Press, 2008.

Banjo, Shelly. "Middle Schools Fail Kids, Study Says," *Wall Street Journal*, September 1, 2010. Retrieved March 2012 (http://online.wsj.com/article/SB10001424052748704421104575464151699794576.html).

Brown, David F., and Trudy Knowles. *What Every Middle School Teacher Should Know.* Portsmouth, NH: Heinemann, 2007.

Bruzzese, Joe. *Parent's Guide to the Middle School Years.* Berkley, CA: Ten Speed Press, 2009.

Canfield, Jack, et al. *Teens Talk Middle School: 101 Stories of Life, Love, and Learning for Younger Teens* (Chicken Soup for the Soul). Cos Cob, CT: Chicken Soup for the Soul, 2008.

Duncan, Arne. "The New Consensus on Middle-Grades Reform." U.S. Department of Education, November 10, 2011. Retrieved March 2012 (http://www.ed.gov/news/speeches/new-consensus-middle-grade-reform).

Kutcher, Martin, and Marcella Moran. *Organizing the Disorganized Child: Simple Strategies to Succeed in School.* New York, NY: HarperCollins Publishers, 2009.

National Center for Education Statistics. "Digest of Education Statistics." 2010. Retrieved March 2012 (http://nces.ed.gov/programs/digest).

Parks, Jerry L. *Teacher Under Construction: Things I Wish I'd Known: A Survival Handbook for New Middle School Teachers.* Lincoln, NE: Weekly Reader Press, 2004.

Pickhardt, Carl. *Why Good Kids Act Cruel: The Hidden Truth About the Pre-Teen Years.* Napierville, IL: Sourcebooks, Inc., 2010.

Puckett, David. *Tips for Surviving & Thriving Through the Middle School Years: A Guide for Teachers & Parents.* Nashville, TN: Incentive Publications, 2011.

Stacha, Adria (school counselor, Hassler Elementary, Klein I.S.D, Spring, TX), in discussion with the author, November 2011.

index